SIMPLE
TIPS
FOR
Gardeners

Written and compiled by Rachel Quillin.

ISBN 978-1-60260-703-3

Scripture quotations are taken from the King James version of the Bible.

Published by Barbour Publishing, Inc., P.O. Box 719, Uhrichsville, Ohio 44683, www.barbourbooks.com

Our mission is to publish and distribute inspirational products offering exceptional value and biblical encouragement to the masses.

Member of the
Evangelical Christian
Publishers Association

Printed in China.

SIMPLE
TIPS
FOR
Gardeners

BARBOUR
PUBLISHING

The kiss of the sun for pardon,
The song of the birds
for mirth,
One is nearer God's heart
in a garden
Than anywhere else
on earth.

"GARDEN THOUGHTS,"
DOROTHY FRANCES GURNEY

My green thumb came only as a result of the mistakes I made while learning to see things from the plant's point of view.

H. Fred Ale

$\mathcal{G}$ardening is civil and social, but it wants the vigor and freedom of the forest and the outlaw.

Henry David Thoreau

SEEDS

To save money, consider growing your annuals from seeds rather than cell packs. You will probably have more seeds than you will need, so set up a seed exchange with other gardeners who are starting their own plants.

THE RIGHT SPOT

Find the right spot for each plant.
Group types of plants by their
needs so you can take care of
a particular chore at one
time and place.

GOOD ROOT GROWTH

*U*se organic fertilizers for
perennials to support root
development and soil-borne
organisms that are good
for root growth.

There is no spot of ground,
however arid, bare, or ugly, that
cannot be tamed into such a state as
may give an impression of
beauty and delight.

GERTRUDE JEKYLL

*G*od made rainy days so the gardeners could get the housework done.

UNKNOWN

NEAT AND NEW

Deadheading might not be the most exciting gardening task, but the rewards of neat-looking gardens and new growth are well worth it.

$\mathcal{L}$ove is like dew that falls on both nettles and lilies.

SWEDISH PROVERB

And the LORD God took the man, and put him into the garden of Eden to dress it and to keep it.

GENESIS 2:15

*G*ardening requires lots
of water—most of it in the
form of perspiration.

LOU ERICKSON

PEST CONTROL

Do you find yourself fighting garden pests regularly? To help identify the pest correctly, check with someone at your local extension office or a garden nursery. They will help you decide what means of pest control—whether chemical or organic— will be most effective.

EDGING OPTIONS

*G*arden edging is important for defining boundaries and keeping your lawn from growing into your garden. Some good edging options include a simple trench, metal or plastic edging, or flagstone or concrete pavers.

MID-SUMMER SPRUCING

*M*id-summer will probably find your garden needing some sprucing up. Cut back plants that look poor. Deadhead where needed. Add fresh annuals or potted plants where you find obvious holes. Spend a little extra time weeding and watering and maybe add a new statue or birdhouse.

I have never had so many good ideas day after day as when I worked in the garden.

JOHN ERSKINE

BOUNDARIES

One way to make your garden easier to control is to use raised garden beds or containers. This gives your garden definite boundaries.

*T*he watering of a garden requires
as much judgment as the
seasoning of a soup.

HELENA RUTHERFORD ELY

LATE FALL

Late fall is a good time to move woody plants or to plant trees or shrubs. Be sure to use tree guards to protect young trees.

Keep a green tree in your heart and perhaps a singing bird will come.

CHINESE PROVERB

MULCH BENEFITS

Mulch is very important. It is more than a garden decoration. It keeps roots cool and helps prevent weeds from growing, making less work for you in the garden.

$\mathcal{A}$ single rose can be my garden. . .
a single friend, my world.

LEO F. BUSCAGLIA

CUTTING ROSES

*C*ut back roses in early
spring. . .not in the fall.

Take seed-starting a step further and become a seed saver. Only open pollinated plants will grow true from seed, but there are probably plenty of them in your garden.

MARIE IANNOTTI

*O*f all the wonderful things in the wonderful universe of God, nothing seems to me more surprising than the planting of a seed in the blank earth and the result thereof.

JULIE MOIR MESSERVY

They that sow in tears shall reap in joy. He that goeth forth and weepeth, bearing precious seed, shall doubtless come again with rejoicing, bringing his sheaves with him.

PSALM 126:5–6

There can be no other occupation like gardening in which, if you were to creep up behind someone at their work, you would find them smiling.

MIRABEL OSLER

WAGONS AND WHEELBARROWS

*I*nvest in a wagon or wheelbarrow.
Use it to haul plants, tools,
mulch. . . . You'll be amazed
at how much more you're
able to accomplish.

GARDENING NECESSITIES

$\mathcal{G}$ardening necessities include a
shovel, trowel, watering can or hose,
and a good weeding tool.
Also purchase good gloves,
a wide-brimmed hat,
and sunscreen.

GARDENING TOOLS

*A*dditional gardening tools good to have on hand are a hoe, good pruners, and a hand cultivator.

$\mathcal{T}$ruths are first clouds; then rain,
then harvest and food.

HENRY WARD BEECHER

PLANT SWAPPING

*C*onsider a plant swap in the spring when you are dividing plants. You and your friends will have a wonderful time sharing tidbits about the plants you are exchanging, and you'll create beautiful gardens and wonderful memories.

$\mathcal{W}$here flowers bloom
so does hope.

LADY BIRD JOHNSON

I do not think I have ever seen anything more beautiful than the bluebell I have been looking at. I know the beauty of our Lord by it.

GERARD MANLEY HOPKINS

GARDEN VARIETY

To create an attractive display in your flower gardens, use a variety of heights, widths, and colors that appeal to you.

$\mathcal{L}$et us be grateful to people who make us happy; they are the charming gardeners who make our souls blossom.

MARCEL PROUST

BE AWARE...

*W*hen gardening around children's play areas, be aware that some common plants are quite poisonous. These include Chinese Lantern Plant or Strawberry ground-cherry (ripened fruits are edible, but unripened fruits and leaves are poisonous), Chrysanthemum (skin irritant), Hydrangea, Lantana, Rhododendron, and Azalea.

CONTAINER GARDENING

Wanting to try container gardening? Think creatively, and nearly anything can become a container. Try old boots, washtubs, barrels, bowls, pitchers, and mugs. You can even use water-based paints to decorate items like milk jugs and use those for containers. Visit garage sales and flea markets for inspiration.

LET THE SUNSHINE IN

*I*f you want to plant an indoor garden, you need to consider the light source. Choose your plants accordingly.

*E*very child is born a naturalist.
His eyes are, by nature, open to the
glories of the stars, the beauty of
the flowers, and the mystery of life.

R. SEARCH

$\mathcal{B}$e not deceived; God is not mocked: for whatsoever a man soweth, that shall he also reap.

GALATIANS 6:7

The best place to seek God is in a garden. You can dig for Him there.

GEORGE BERNARD SHAW

IN BULK

*B*uy things such as mulch, fertilizer,
and plant stakes in bulk
to save money.

VEGETABLE GARDENING

$\mathcal{W}$hen choosing a spot for a vegetable garden, pick a sunny place close to the house. This will give you easier access when you need to work in it, and when it's time to harvest, the job will be done more easily.

*C*hildren usually spend more time in the garden than anybody else. It is where they learn about the world, because they can be in it unsupervised, yet protected. Some gardeners will remember from their own earliest recollections that no one sees the garden as vividly, or cares about it as passionately, as the child who grows up in it.

CAROL WILLIAMS

*I*n the spring, at the end of the day,
you should smell like dirt.

MARGARET ATWOOD

BEGINNING GARDENER

If you are a novice vegetable gardener, select plants that grow easily, such as beans and corn. Gradually add more challenging plants.

ROTATE

$\mathcal{P}$ut plant rotation into practice when planning your garden each year. Your carrots will thrive with the nutrients left behind from last year's beans.

SALES AND PROMOS

Take advantage of catalog sales and use the promotions to try something like peanuts or a new herb you normally wouldn't plant.

One of the greatest virtues of
gardening is this perpetual renewal
of youth and spring, of promise
of flower and fruit that can always
be read in the open book of the
garden, by those with an eye to see,
and a mind to understand.

E. A. Bowles

TAG IT

To remember which plant you want to move, tag it while it is still in bloom. That way you are sure to move the correct one.

$\mathcal{A}$ man should never plant a garden larger than his wife can take care of.

T. H. EVERETT

$\mathcal{N}$one can have a healthy love for
flowers unless he loves
the wild ones.

Forbes Watson

WEEDING ADVICE

When weeding your flowers or
vegetables, be sure to pull the weed
out by the root so that
it won't regrow.

*N*othing is more the child of art than a garden.

Sir Walter Scott

A sower went out to sow his seed
. . . . And other fell on good ground,
and sprang up, and bare fruit an
hundredfold. And when he had said
these things, he cried, He that hath
ears to hear, let him hear.

LUKE 8:5, 8

The greatest gift of the garden is the restoration of the five senses.

HANNA RION

GARDEN LAYOUT

The tags on your plants are there
for a reason. Pay attention to the
height and spacing directions when
you are planning the layout
for your garden.

LITTLE WATER

*I*f you want beautiful flowers but don't want to spend a lot of time watering your garden, look for gorgeous plants that require little water.

*C*onfess yourself to heaven,
Repent what's past, avoid
what is to come,
And do not spread the
compost on the weeds
To make them ranker.

SHAKESPEARE

COMPOST

$\mathcal{D}$on't let garden cleanup or fallen leaves go to waste. Create compost! It makes great fertilizer for your garden.

TAKE ADVANTAGE OF
THE WEATHER

$\mathcal{W}$ater your flower garden area the day before you plant or plant the day after it rains. Pay attention to the weather forecast, and choose a cloudy, cooler day to ward off stress for you and the plants.

START SMALL

When designing your first flower garden, start small. Consider the amount of light available in the spot you select, and choose low-maintenance plants.

$\mathcal{D}$o not anticipate trouble or worry about what may never happen. Keep in the sunlight

BENJAMIN FRANKLIN

$\mathcal{P}$raise is like sunlight to the
human spirit: we cannot flower
and grow without it.

JES LAIR

$\mathcal{T}$oo old to plant trees for my own
gratification, I shall do it
for my posterity.

THOMAS JEFFERSON

ROSE CARE

Roses require about eight hours of
sunlight each day; and the morning
hours are best, so consider this
when choosing a spot for
your rose plants.

PERENNIAL SEEDS

$\mathcal{D}$on't be afraid to leave perennial seed heads in your garden once the season ends. They will add interest to your winter garden, and you will have more seeds when the next season arrives.

BEAUTIFUL DISPLAY

*M*ix and match. A variety of
types of roses such as bushes,
climbing roses, and tea roses make
a beautiful display. Also add other
items of interest, such as barrels
and trellises.

Some people are always grumbling
because roses have thorns. I am
thankful that thorns have roses.

ALPHONSE KERR

The fruit of the righteous is a tree of life; and he that winneth souls is wise.

PROVERBS 11:30

In my garden there is a large place
for sentiment. My garden of
flowers is also my garden of
thoughts and dreams.
The thoughts grow as freely
as the flowers, and the
dreams are as beautiful.

ABRAM L. URBAN

OLD NEWSPAPER USE

*U*se shredded newspapers for
weed barriers or to hold
moisture in the bottom
of potted plants.

ROSE FOOD

*U*se specialized rose food as fertilizer for your roses.

$\mathcal{B}$ut he that dares not grasp the thorn should never crave the rose.

ANNE BRONTË

The many great gardens of the world, of literature and poetry, of painting and music, of religion and architecture, all make the point as clear as possible: The soul cannot thrive in the absence of a garden. If you don't want paradise, you are not human; and if you are not human, you don't have a soul.

THOMAS MOORE

INSECT PREVENTION

$\mathcal{B}$ecause fruit trees attract beetles and insects, it is important to use insecticides to prevent infestation. Check with your extension office to decide on an insecticide that is environmentally friendly as well as effective.

$\mathcal{J}$udge a tree from its fruit,
not from its leaves.

EURIPIDES

PATIENCE REQUIRED

Try a variety of fruit trees, bushes, and plants to make your property attractive and valuable, but be patient. It takes more time for fruit trees to produce than other types of plants.

$\mathcal{W}$ishing to be friends is quick work, but friendship is a slow-ripening fruit.

ARISTOTLE

INTERESTING APPEAL

Use broken statues or ceramics that
you have glued back together to
add interesting visual appeal
to your garden.

PRUNING

Fruit trees will need to be pruned to stay healthy, but if you are unsure of how to do this pay an expert the first few times you do it. It's worth the cost to protect your tree.

S ometimes our fate resembles a fruit tree in winter. Who would think that those branches would turn green again and blossom, but we hope it, we know it.

JOHANN WOLFGANG VON GOETHE

BARRELS

Some smaller fruits, such as strawberries, will do well when grown in barrels. This is attractive and will save some time in your garden care.

The most noteworthy thing about gardeners is that they are always optimistic, always enterprising, and never satisfied. They always look forward to doing something better than they have ever done before.

VITA SACKVILLE-WEST

$\mathcal{B}$ut the fruit of the Spirit is love, joy, peace, longsuffering, gentleness, goodness, faith, meekness, temperance: against such there is no law.

GALATIANS 5:22–23

I used to visit and revisit it a dozen times a day, and stand in deep contemplation over my vegetable progeny with a love that nobody could share or conceive of who had never taken part in the process of creation. It was one of the most bewitching sights in the world to observe a hill of beans thrusting aside the soil, or a rose of early peas just peeping forth sufficiently to trace a line of delicate green.

NATHANIEL HAWTHORNE

FLOWERBED PREP

Start in the fall to prepare a new flowerbed for the following spring. Choose the space you want for your garden and outline the shape using a garden hose or landscape chalk. Cover the area well with black and white newspapers. Wet down the newspapers to hold them in place. Cover the area with bagged or organic potting soil. Begin to think about the plants you want there the following spring.

TALL GARDEN PLANTS

Remember that taller plants might need to be staked, especially if you live in a windy area.

The tree of silence bears the fruit of peace.

Arabian Proverb

$\mathcal{D}$on't throw away the old bucket
until you know if the new
one holds water.

SWEDISH PROVERB

HOMEMADE SOIL SIFTERS

*M*ake soil sifters from old leaky buckets. Cut the bottoms, leaving about a ½-inch "ledge" around the base. Attach a circle of ¼- or ½-inch hardware cloth to the inside of the bucket, in drilled holes, with pop rivets or small nuts and bolts with washers. These are great for removing trash from potting soil and compost.

ROCK GARDENS

$\mathcal{R}$ock gardens are beautiful, but they do require a bit of research and planning. Make sure you choose a sloping area that is near a natural or artificial stream.

KITS

$\mathcal{R}$ock garden kits can be purchased at your local garden center and should have all that you need to make your rock garden a success.

$\mathcal{P}$luck the weeds from your
patch of dreams.

UNKNOWN

One of the most important resources that a garden makes available for use, is the gardener's own body. A garden gives the body the dignity of working in its own support. It is a way of rejoining the human race.

WENDELL BERRY

ADDING ATTRACTION

When you are planning your gardens, remember that their purpose is to make your home more attractive—not to hide it.

In the dooryard fronting an
old farmhouse near the
white-wash'd palings,
Stands the lilac-bush tall-growing
with heart-shaped leaves
of rich green, with many a
pointed blossom rising delicate,
with the perfume strong I love,
With every leaf a miracle—and from
this bush in the dooryard,
With delicate-color'd blossoms and
heart-shaped leaves of rich green,
A sprig with its flower I break.

WALT WHITMAN

*B*otanically speaking, tomatoes
are the fruit of a vine, just as are
cucumbers, squashes,
beans, and peas.

HORACE GRAY

CONTAIN INVASIVE PLANTS

Some plants are beautiful but invasive. If you want to include them in your garden simply cut out the bottom of a plastic pot and sink the pot in the ground to its rim. Fill the pot with soil and put the plant in the pot.

I am the vine, ye are the branches: He that abideth in me, and I in him, the same bringeth forth much fruit: for without me ye can do nothing.

JOHN 15:5

Take thy plastic spade,
It is thy pencil;
Take thy seeds, thy plants,
They are thy colours.

WILLIAM MASON

CAREFUL PLANNING

$\mathcal{B}$e careful where you place bushes and trees. Consider things such as power lines and buildings that the mature plant will affect.

FUTURE GARDEN

Consider the future when planning your gardens. You don't want any unwelcome surprises to cause problems because of improper planning.

LOW-MAINTENANCE GARDEN

$\mathcal{W}$ater gardens are beautiful and require a bit less maintenance than traditional gardens, but do not overfeed fish or over-fertilize your plants. If you do, you will be sure to encounter an algae problem.

*L*aying out grounds may be considered a liberal art, in some sort like poetry and painting.

WILLIAM WORDSWORTH

Happy in all that ragged, loose collapse of water, the fountain, its effortless descent and flatteries of spray...

RICHARD WILBUR

DIRECT SUNLIGHT

$\mathcal{P}$lace your water garden where it will receive plenty of light, as the plants and fish both require much direct sunlight.

GOING ORGANIC

*I*f you want to garden organically, create your own compost instead of adding chemical fertilizer. Also add pine needles, grass clippings, and shredded newspaper as mulch.

The Earth laughs in flowers.

RALPH WALDO EMERSON

BUTTERFLIES

$\mathcal{B}$utterflies are attracted to certain plants, but they also need a shallow water source to be content in a garden. Consider a shallow bowl or lid for them to stop and get a drink.

SEEDLING POTS

$\mathcal{U}$se cardboard tubes to create pots for seedlings. Clip one end and fold it in to create a bottom. Transplants can be planted directly into the ground with the tube left on. The cardboard will disintegrate faster than a regular peat pot.

GARDEN ATTIRE

*C*hoose comfortable, form-fitting clothing and shoes for garden work. This will make your gardening pleasant and safe.

$\mathcal{W}$hat's in a name? that
which we call a rose
By any other name
would smell as sweet.

SHAKESPEARE

SCIENTIFIC NAMES

$\mathcal{D}$o a little reading and learn the
scientific names for the plants you
love. This will help ensure that you
purchase the correct plants.

Say not ye, There are yet four months, and then cometh harvest? behold, I say unto you, Lift up your eyes, and look on the fields; for they are white already to harvest.

JOHN 4:35

$Gardening$ is about enjoying the
smell of things growing in the soil,
getting dirty without feeling guilty,
and generally taking the time to
soak up a little peace and serenity.

LINDLEY KARSTENS

SOIL

$\mathcal{L}$earn the soil pH that your vegetables require. This will help you determine where to plant each vegetable and what you need to add to the soil.

IDEAL SOIL

Sandy loam is the best type of soil for vegetable gardening. Try squeezing your soil into a ball and watching to see if it crumbles. If you can do this, you have ideal soil.

*I*f a healthy soil is full of death,
it is also full of life: worms, fungi,
microorganisms of all kinds. . . .
Given only the health of the
soil, nothing that dies is
dead for very long.

WENDELL BERRY

ORGANIC MULCH

Use mulch made from organic matter such as cocoa hulls, shredded bark, or compost. This will ward off weeds as well as add nutrients to your soil.

If I wanted to have a happy garden, I must ally myself with my soil; study and help it to the utmost, untiringly. . . . Always, the soil must come first.

MARION CRAN

GARDEN PLANNING
HOMEWORK

$\mathcal{D}$o your homework! Before you begin your garden, find out which plants are well adapted to your area of the country. It is also important to know how much and what kind of care the plant will require. Also consider how much time you will have to put into a garden, as well.

*O*pportunity is missed by most people because it is dressed in overalls and looks like work.

THOMAS A. EDISON

TOMATO PLANT CARE

After you make hard-boiled eggs,
let the water cool. Pour the water
around your tomato plants to
prevent calcium deficiency.

EASIER WATERING

*U*se a soaker hose attached to a timer to use less water and to make watering an easier task.

YOUNG WEEDS

*W*eeds are easier to pull when they are young, and it also prevents them from reproducing.

To enjoy freedom. . .we have of
course to control ourselves.
We must not squander our powers,
helplessly and ignorantly, squirting
half the house in order to
water a single rose.

VIRGINIA WOOLF

FLAT EDGING

*W*hen you edge your gardens, consider using a flat edging. That way the wheels of your mower can go right over it and make the task that much easier.

These are the hands whose
sturdy labor brings
The peasant's food, the
golden pomp of kings. . .
These are the lines that
heaven-commanded
Toil shows on his deed,
—the charter of the soil!

OLIVER WENDELL HOLMES

Blessed is the man that walketh not in the counsel of the ungodly, nor standeth in the way of sinners, nor sitteth in the seat of the scornful. But his delight is in the law of the LORD; and in his law doth he meditate day and night. And he shall be like a tree planted by the rivers of water, that bringeth forth his fruit in his season; his leaf also shall not wither; and whatsoever he doeth shall prosper.

PSALM 1:1–3

$\mathcal{H}$ow fair is a garden amid the
trials and passions of existence.

BENJAMIN DISRAELI

RAISED FLOWER BEDS

If you are using raised flower beds, build them small enough so that you can easily reach them from both sides without having to walk through them.

There are two lasting bequests we can give our children: one is roots. The other is wings.

HODDING CARTER JR.

KIDS' GARDENING

$\mathcal{W}$ant to get your kids interested in gardening? Try a sunflower hideout or a bean teepee. If your space is limited, let them paint flowerpots and create a container garden.

GARDEN TOOL EFFICIENCY

To make your gardening tools more efficient, sharpen them or have them sharpened each spring.

I once had a sparrow alight upon my shoulder for a moment, while I was hoeing in a village garden, and I felt that I was more distinguished by that circumstance than I should have been by any epaulet I could have worn.

HENRY DAVID THOREAU

EARLY TOMATO PROTECTION

*U*se twenty-pound cat litter jugs to cover early tomatoes. Remove the bottom of the jug, and either remove the cap or drill a few holes in the cap to prevent the tomatoes from overheating.

TIME

Plan your garden according to the amount of time you have to spend in it. You can always add to it later if you find you have more time.

Gardening is any way that humans and nature come together with the intent of creating beauty.

TINA JAMES

COMMUNITY GARDENS

$\mathcal{W}$hy not share your love of gardening with others by organizing a community garden? It's a wonderful way to bring the community together and to provide a sense of well-being for everyone involved. Just be sure to research first and form a planning committee to make sure that your garden is well thought-out.

I am of the opinion that my life belongs to the whole community and as long as I live, it is my privilege to do for it whatever I can. I want to be thoroughly used up when I die, for the harder I work the more I live.

GEORGE BERNARD SHAW

$\mathcal{T}$he impersonal hand of government can never replace the helping hand of a neighbor.

HUBERT H. HUMPHREY

COMMUNITY GARDEN PROS

The wonderful benefits of a community garden include bringing the community together, creating a natural space in city neighborhoods, teaching children about where their food comes from, and providing a place for people to grow their own foods.

HERB GARDENS

$\mathcal{H}$erbs are a great option for
container gardening, and the
results add a lot of pizzazz to your
cooking. Just use a good container
and potting mix, and
never over-fertilize.

*H*ow goodly are thy tents, O Jacob,
and thy tabernacles, O Israel!
As the valleys are they spread forth,
as gardens by the river's side, as the
trees of lign aloes which the LORD
hath planted, and as cedar trees
beside the waters.

NUMBERS 24:5–6

*O*ur England is a garden, and such
gardens are not made
By singing: "Oh, how beautiful!"
and sitting in the shade.

RUDYARD KIPLING

COOL-WEATHER PLANTS

When spring fever sets in and you just can't stay out of the garden, be sure to choose plants that are suited to cooler weather. Lettuce and snow peas are a good option.

There is a garden in every childhood, an enchanted place where colors are brighter, the air softer, and the morning more fragrant than ever again.

ELIZABETH LAWRENCE

LEARNING OPPORTUNITIES

Give children hands-on history
lessons by teaching them how
to create corn husk dolls and
brooms from broom corn.
Hands-on science lessons are
great, too, as they collect and
learn about different bugs and
insects, types of plants,
plant care, etc.

PREVENTING WASTE

Space out the dates of lettuce planting, or your whole crop will be ready to harvest at the same time, and much of it will be wasted.

EXTENDED GROWING SEASON

Hotbeds and cold frames are great
ways to extend the growing season
of your vegetable gardens.

$\mathcal{L}$ove is the only flower that grows
and blossoms
Without the aid of the seasons.

KAHLIL GIBRAN

GARDENING SUPPLY STEALS

*Y*ard sales are a wonderful place to find gardening supplies such as tools, pots, or buckets.

As for marigolds, poppies, hollyhocks, and valorous sunflowers, we shall never have a garden without them, both for their own sake, and for the sake of old-fashioned folks, who used to love them.

Henry Ward Beecher

HEIRLOOM VEGGIES

*T*ry heirloom vegetables. They are the "real" thing—not hybrids. They are open-pollinated, can be traced back at least fifty years, and their seeds were saved by particular families or ethnic groups. They are a little easier to obtain now as many seed catalogs carry them.

$\mathcal{Y}$our mind is a garden,
your thoughts are the seeds,
the harvest can be either
flowers or weeds.

UNKNOWN

GARDEN JOURNAL

Keep a garden journal. Include when and where your plants are planted, temperatures and rainfall or watering schedule, pests and welcomed creatures that have arrived. . . . If you are feeling especially creative or expressive, include pictures of your garden or add poetry. You might also want to include a section of "garden dreams" and ideas that you have taken from magazines or found in other gardens.

THEME IDEAS

When planning your various garden themes, look at photos in magazines, books, and newspapers to help you come up with ideas.

LIMITED SPACE

Water features don't have to be large. If your space is limited, try a small fountain or even a birdbath.

I made me gardens and orchards, and I planted trees in them of all kind of fruits.

ECCLESIASTES 2:5

Gardening is the art that uses flowers and plants as paint, and the soil and sky as canvas.

ELIZABETH MURRAY

Earth knows no desolation.
She smells regeneration in
the moist breath of decay.

GEORGE MEREDITH

KITCHEN SCRAPS

Save your kitchen scraps in a lightly covered bucket. Do not include meat, and be sure to crush egg shells and chop up peelings. Once a week take your scraps and work it into the aisles of your garden. It creates a wonderful compost and eliminates the need for bins and barrels in your yard. Next season alternate your rows so that your plants are where your compost was and vice versa.

SHADE GARDENS

SHADY AREAS

Shade gardens are a great possibility if you enrich the soil and choose plants such as hostas and impatiens that thrive in shady areas.

$\mathcal{T}$o sit in the shade on a fine day
and look upon verdure is the most
perfect refreshment.

JANE AUSTEN

COFFEE GROUNDS

$\mathcal{M}$any people like to use fresh coffee grounds around plants, but it's important to remember that all plants won't respond the same to this addition to their soil. Use fresh grounds sparingly, and mix the rest with your compost.

COFFEE GROUND BENEFITS

There are many pluses to the addition of coffee grounds in your garden. They keep ants, snails, and slugs at bay; but they attract worms, which are very beneficial to your garden.

COMPOST ADDITION

*A*nimal manure can be a real bonus to your compost, but don't add fresh manure where plants are growing. It will burn them.

Over-fertilized plants may be beautiful but are otherwise useless, like people whose energies are devoted so completely to their appearance that there is no other development.

WILLIAM LONGGOOD

WATERING ECONOMICS

*C*onsider using a rain barrel to save money and water or install drip irrigation.

*W*ater sustains all.

THALES OF MILETUS

RECIPE TIPS

*I*t always seems that it's wintertime when I find great recipes utilizing fresh vegetables. Then when the vegetables are fresh in my garden, the recipes are gone. The solution: Put each recipe in a page protector. Arrange them by vegetable type in a three-ring binder, so that when you need to use up those extra zucchini, tomatoes, and beans, you know where to turn.

*I*t's difficult to think anything but pleasant thoughts while eating a homegrown tomato.
LEWIS GRIZZARD

REGULAR ATTENTION

Pay attention to your garden. Walk through it every few days, and take care of problems as soon as possible. Stay ahead of it to get the most out of it.

𝒜wake, O north wind; and come, thou south; blow upon my garden, that the spices thereof may flow out. Let my beloved come into his garden, and eat his pleasant fruits.

SONG OF SOLOMON 4:16

$\mathcal{A}$ll through the long winter, I dream of my garden. On the first day of spring, I dig my fingers deep into the soft earth. I can feel its energy, and my spirits soar.

Helen Hayes

WORKING TOGETHER

𝓛earn as much as possible about what plants work together well to benefit the entire garden. Did you know that it's a good idea to plant roses and garlic together?

THE FIVE SENSES

When planning your garden, consider that it should appeal to all five senses. Add plants with great colors, scents, and textures. Add something edible and features such as wind chimes or a water fountain for relaxing sounds.

THEMED PLANTS

Depending on how involved you want your garden to be, you might want to add themed plants to your landscapes. Possibilities include butterfly or bird gardens, wildlife gardens, perennial gardens, shade gardens, Japanese gardens, formal gardens, water gardens, etc. The possibilities are truly endless.

$\mathcal{W}$eather means more when you
have a garden. There's nothing like
listening to a shower and thinking
how it is soaking in around
your green beans.

MARCELENE COX

TIMELY PLANTING

*M*ake sure you research the proper
time of year for planting
a particular plant.

$\mathcal{A}$ pool is the eye of the garden in whose candid depths is mirrored its advancing grace.

LOUISE BEBE WILDER

LOCAL LIBRARY

𝒜 valuable but often overlooked source of gardening information is your local library. You will find books, magazines, DVDs. . .on all types of plants, gardening design, care, etc. You are likely to find new ideas on things you've never considered trying. If the library doesn't have what you are looking for, they should be able to get it for you through interlibrary loan.

How often it is that a garden, beautiful though it be, will seem sad and dreary and lacking in one of its most gracious features, if it has no water.

PIERRE HUSSON

PERENNIALS

*W*hen planning a perennial garden, think about how many plants you want to include, as well as how many you'd like to use for cut flowers, and plant your flowers accordingly. Also research what plants make good dried flower arrangements, as they make lovely gifts and additions to your home decor.